I0409970

TABLE OF CONTENTS

INTRODUCTION

"The United States of America is fighting a war against terrorists of global reach. The enemy is not a single political regime or person or religion or ideology. The enemy is terrorism—premeditated, politically motivated violence perpetrated against innocents."

"The struggle against global terrorism is different from any other war in our history"[1]

This excerpt from our current National Security Strategy is a frank description of just how different America's global war on terrorism was predicted to be following the September 11th 2001 Al Qa'eda attacks on Washington and New York, and is equally as telling of the challenges which lay ahead. Perhaps the most striking difference between this conflict and those of the past is the nature of the enemy. America is not fighting a regime or ideology as it did in nearly every other conflict in the past. There is no "evil empire" manifested in Soviet communism, no "Aryan solution" as pursued by Adolph Hitler's Third Reich, no ethnic cleansing regime to eradicate or fragmented nation to reunite. This is quite literally a war against a *means* of waging war vice the *ends* to which a war is fought.

In his address to Congress shortly after the 9-11 attacks, President George W. Bush avowed that the war on terrorism will not end until "every terrorist group of global reach has been found, stopped and defeated."[2] Needless to say, to achieve that desired end state in this war will undoubtedly require innovative and aggressive employment of <u>all</u> elements of national power, and not necessarily in the military-centric thinking that exemplified previous conflicts. Furthermore, such a prolonged and comprehensive

---

[1] *The National Security Strategy of the United States of America*, Washington DC, 2002, p 5.

[2] George W. Bush, Address to Congress, Washington DC, 20 Sep 2001.

1

conflict will demand the patience and support of not only the American people, but also the unprecedented support of all nations engaged in this fight.

At this moment, America's war on terror is being waged in multiple theaters worldwide and, concurrently, is aimed at destroying (or reducing to ineffectiveness) the traditional critical strengths and weaknesses of the Al Qa'eda terrorist network. During Operation ENDURING FREEDOM in Afghanistan since late-2001, the United States has and continues to target the global terrorist group Al Qa'eda, more specifically its safe haven under Taliban rule, and its leadership under Sheikh Usama Bin Laden. Elsewhere, the U.S. government has sought (often successfully) to freeze Al Qa'eda's financial assets worldwide as well as to exploit the organization's far flung command and control system so as to intercept intelligence on future operations and apprehend individuals or terrorist cells.

Unarguably, this multi-pronged attack on Al Qa'eda is classic Clausewitz and even though terrorism by nature is primarily tactical action with strategic results, thereby skipping the operational level of warfare, fighting back at the tactical and strategic levels can still employ significant operational art principles. Through careful analysis, it is generally acceptable that the key areas of leadership, sanctuary, finance and C2 can be viewed as critical strengths and/or weaknesses, and all vulnerable for targeting by the U.S. and its allies. Indeed a cornerstone of the current National Strategy for Defeating Terrorism (*Defeat*-Deny-Diminish-Defend), attacking a terrorist organization's sanctuaries, leadership, material support, financial base and C2 will "have a cascading effect across the larger terrorist landscape, disrupting the terrorists' ability to plan and operate."[3] Or will it? Certainly, it is evident by this point in Operation ENDURING FREEDOM, neither the removal of the Taliban as Al Qa'eda's protectorate body nor the relative marginalization of Usama Bin Laden in the Tora Bora caves has significantly degraded that organization's ability to carry out operations. At this time, Al Qa'eda continues to successfully mount coordinated attacks, such as those against what was then *believed* to be U.S. housing compounds in Riyadh, Saudi Arabia, in 2003. Furthermore, continued Al Qa'eda and related terrorist "chatter" has been credited with routinely raising the Department of Homeland Security's National Threat Level several times since 2001.

Defeating global terrorism will require more than the targeting and destruction of the many terrorist organizations and their reconstitutable factors. The true center of gravity of any terrorist organization is its linkage with its constituency, whether real or perceived, and THAT linkage is made through the organization's message. Without the support of an audience, a terrorist or a terrorist organization is destined to "die on the vine." The true test for the United States in its war on terror will be how it employs its elements of national power, i.e. the power of diplomacy, information superiority, military force and economic incentive (or penalty), to de-legitimize a terror organization's message to potential supporters and recruits. Moreover, it must do so without exposing its own COG, the uncompromising support of the American people, to the negative effects of a prolonged and slow paced conflict. Tangible factors are almost always reconstitutable over time, but an organization's message, once discredited, is seldom resurrected. In the case of Al Qa'eda, its message of hate towards the United States, its

---

[3] *National Strategy for Combating Terrorism*, Washington DC, p 11.

allies and other moderate Muslim regimes is a thinly-veiled distortion of Islamic beliefs. In truth, Bin Laden's message is ripe for dissection by legitimate Islamic scholars, who can easily discredit Al Qa'eda's mission using the same Muslim laws. They only need a reason to do so—America should take the lead in providing that reason.

This paper will focus on a terrorist's center of gravity, his message. Primary attention will be given to the current campaign against Al Qa'eda in America's global war on terrorism. Furthermore, the paper will illustrate that despite the apparent lack of an operational level in this war, Clausewitzian fundamentals and operational art remain key elements in securing ultimate victory in this "new kind of war."[4] We cannot enjoy a permanent peace unless we win a "war of ideas… to make clear that all acts of terrorism are illegitimate … viewed in the same light as slavery, piracy and genocide."[5]

OPERATIONAL DESIGN: CRITICAL FACTORS

As mentioned, terrorism tends to be actions conducted at the tactical level of warfare which, when successfully carried out, tends to have strategic implications or might draw strategic reactions. Nevertheless, operational art still plays a central role in planning and execution, serving as the foundation upon which rational employment of national power can be projected.[6] Properly identified critical factors and center(s) of gravity, whether tangible or intangible, will enable the U.S. to focus its instruments of power upon Al Qa'eda's source of political and social leverage.[7] In particular, it is doubtful that Karl Von Clausewitz ever considered such a conflict when he published *On*

---

[4] George W. Bush, Address, The National Cathedral, Washington DC, 14 Sep 2001.

[5] *National Strategy for Combating Terrorism*, Washington DC, p 23.

[6] Milan Vego, *Operational Warfare*, Newport RI, Naval War College Press, 2000, p 309.

[7] Ibid.

War and formulated his principle of center of gravity (COG) in warfare between belligerent nations. His postulation of center of gravity was derived literally from the physical science definition, i.e. the point where the forces of gravity converge within an object, or in military terms, "the hub of all power and movement on which everything depends."[8] Yet, arguably in every previous case, that enemy center of gravity, be it one or many, was a tangible and targetable entity. How does one now reconcile the concept of center of gravity to an enemy who may at times not have an army, or a base, or capital weapons, or a state to call its own? The answer to this question beckons back to Dr. Milan Vego's generic definition of COG: a "source of massed strength—physical or moral—whose serious degradation, dislocation, neutralization or destruction would have the most decisive impact on the [enemy.]"[9] As this definition implies, COG is drawn from one's vulnerable critical strengths, not weaknesses. In the case of Al Qa'eda, as with nearly all other terrorist organizations of global reach, five vulnerable critical strengths in particular stand out over all others:

- Charismatic leadership
- Benefit of sanctuary
- Intricate command and control
- Global funding base
- Popular ideology

Leadership. Despite the preponderance of household names like Yassar Arafat, Muammar Quadhafi, the Ayatollah Khomeini or perhaps even Saddam Hussein, all of whom came to personify their causes, the terrorist movements they sponsor (or sponsored at one time) have had a way of enduring despite decapitation or marginalization. It is

---

[8] Michael Howard and Peter Paret, eds., Carl Von Clausewitz (Translated), *On War*, Princeton NJ, Princeton University Press, 1976, p 485.

[9] Vego, 309.

interesting to note the direct translation of Al Qa'eda is "The Base,"[10] which actually came into being as a computer file (by the same name) of those individuals devoutly loyal to Usama Bin Laden through the end of the Soviet occupation of Afghanistan and throughout the 1990's. Usama's name has grown in recent years to become completely synonymous with the Al Qa'eda network and despite repeated admonitions to the contrary, apparently vital to its success as an international organization. Furthermore, he is largely viewed in the (Sunni) Muslim world as one of the most significant unifying forces in recent history.[11] In fact, the structure of Al Qa'eda's core organization appears to underscore his influence across the central Asian continent; the emir-general (Bin Laden) is immediately surrounded by an inner circle of three or four leaders linked to like-minded constituent groups such as the Egyptian Islamic Jihad, the Jamiat-ul-Ulema-e-Pakistan, the Bangladeshi Jihadist Movement and the Kashmiri Harakat-ul-Mujahidin.[12] In establishing a World Islamic Jihad against the Jews and Crusaders through publication of such edicts as 1998 "Fatwah Urging Jihad against Americans," Bin Laden continued to strengthen his influence as the preeminent radical Islamic fundamentalist, and even today, continues to gain support among those with a common hate of U.S. influence and globalization.

While Usama Bin Laden is certainly a credible, if not the *most* credible, foe in the campaign against Al Qa'eda[13], caution should be paid towards focusing too much power and attention in a single direction. Clearly, Bin Laden has carefully orchestrated a

---

[10] Paul R. Pillar, *Terrorism and U.S. Foreign Policy*, Washington DC, Brookings Institute Press, 2001, p 54.

[11] Ibid., 54.

[12] Usama Bin Laden, "Fatwah Urging Jihad Against Americans," 1998.

[13] Pillar, 56.

powerful consensus through clever marketing of his message in the "pan-Islamic" model, drawing support from all corners of the Muslim world, both Arab and non-Arab.[14] The operational links Al Qa'eda shares with other terrorist organizations in the Middle East, Central and Southern Asia, as well as the Far East, serve to galvanize the Usama Bin Laden "culture of personality" amongst his target audience and thus afford him considerable strategic depth. Much to his own validation, eliminating Bin Laden himself, while an important step in diminishing his organization's ability to carry out its mission in the short term (if at all), will have little or no effect on stopping Al Qa'eda's terror campaign in the long run.

Sanctuary. Historically, terrorist organizations have required safe havens in which to base their activities, so as to recruit and train new and existing membership, muster resources (both material and financial) and plan future operations. Certainly in the past, state-sponsorship was a key element in the success of particular organizations, and even today survives albeit in somewhat diminished visibility. [15] Current U.S. policy continues to shine the light on state-sponsored terrorism in that the U.S. will "deny further sponsorship, support and sanctuary to terrorists by ensuring states accept their responsibility to take action against these international threats within their sovereign territory."[16] Where this zero-tolerance warning goes ignored, the U.S. will "act decisively to counter the threat they pose and, ultimately, to compel them to cease

---

[14] 'Combating Terrorism in a Globalized World,' National War College, 2002, ch 2, p9

[15] Six nations are still designated by the State Department as "state sponsors of terrorism," including Cuba, Iran, Libya, North Korea, Syria and Sudan. A seventh, Iraq, is designated as well though this status is certain to change. Source: *Patterns of Global Terrorism*, U.S. Department of State, Washington DC, 2002, p 1.

[16] *National Strategy for Combating Terrorism*, Washington DC, p 11.

supporting terrorism"[17] —perhaps just rhetoric were it not for Operation ENDURING FREEDOM, which clearly demonstrated our resolve to eliminate state-sponsored terrorism in Afghanistan.

Afghanistan, rather, better demonstrates the new direction that global terrorist organizations are taking, seizing control or significant influence over failed/weak states. Those nations or failed states plagued with political unrest, economic failure, insurrection or disaster are fertile grounds for terrorist exploitation, especially the message disseminated by Usama Bin Laden and Al Qa'eda, blaming the United States and its allies for everyone's travails.

Obviously, denying sanctuary forces a terrorist organization to operate in plain view or hostile (to its interests) environment and thus has a negative effect on its freedom of movement. However, like placing all emphasis on targeting terrorist leadership, focusing too much national power at eliminating terrorist safe havens is not enough especially in today's globalized and technologically-interconnected society, and is therefore an unsatisfactory COG. Terrorists and the terrorist organizations of today have the benefit of the Internet and wireless communication, satellite navigation and unprecedented mobility[18], and when coupled with the free and open society of the all-to-often-targeted nation, i.e., the United States, one has found the ultimate sanctuary. There can be no more painful demonstration of this ability than the nineteen (or more) Al Qa'eda operatives, who lived and trained in the U.S. for years before they carried out their horrific mission on September 11th, 2001.

---

[17] Ibid., 12.

[18] Pillar, 48.

Global Finances. Anywhere you go in the world today, one mantra rings true: money turns plans into action, and this is no less true for global terrorist organizations. In fact, funding for many terrorist groups come from a variety of sources, both legal and illegal. Al Qa'eda in particular has been highly successful at raising money through charitable organizations sympathetic to their cause, like-minded wealthy patrons (including Bin Laden himself), international trade of illegal arms, drugs (opium) and minerals ("blood" diamonds), and a host of legitimate, transnational businesses. In fact, Al Qa'eda's *legitimate* profits had been estimated as high as $2.2 **Billion** in banks around the world, including the United States.[19]

Obviously, cutting off that source of money will reduce its ability to carry out its mission, and much headway has been made in this arena. Millions of dollars in foreign assets have been seized in banks around the world and the U.S. has put into action such measures as the Foreign Terrorist Asset Tracking Center to map funding and shut down money laundering schemes wherever possible.[20] Another powerful tool in the U.S. arsenal is the Uniting and Strengthening America by Providing Appropriate Tools Required to Intercept and Obstruct Terrorism (USA PATRIOT) Act, which threatens economic isolation of terrorism-sponsoring nations.[21]

However, the fact remains that terrorism is cheap. It costs relatively little to strap a bomb on and board a bus. And the costs of obtaining flight training in the U.S. were infinitesimally insignificant when compared to the destruction wrought on Sept 11th and the havoc played since. Cutting off Al Qa'eda's finances completely may delay or even

---

[19] 2001 estimate. Yossef Bodansky, *Bin Laden: The Man Who Declared War on America*, New York NY, Prima, 2001, p 314.

[20] 'Combating Terrorism in a Globalized World,' National War College, 2002, ch 5, p 6.

eliminate some operations against the U.S., but the root cause for having an operation in the first place will still smolder over time, waiting to be re-ignited once enough money is raised. Therefore, targeting such a reconstitutable commodity within an organization as its center of gravity would not prove decisive in defeating terrorism in the long run.

Command and Control. Contrary to the popular belief that they are "a bunch of rag-heads riding camels through mountain passes,"[22] in nearly every respect, Al Qa'eda is a modern army.[23] In fact, they use much of the same information technology and communication mediums as are employed by the most advanced armed forces in the world. Al Qa'eda communicates with its operatives throughout the world using satellite phones, cellular communications, internet chat rooms and email, as well as through person-to-person contact. Furthermore, they execute their operations and planning using the best operational security (OPSEC) found anywhere, from routine use of disposable cell phones, to sending/receiving email from anonymous internet cafes and libraries,[24] or employing single-use coded messages in a vast sea of chat rooms or voice traffic.

One might argue that this strength is not necessarily a critical vulnerability on the part of a terrorist organization. Not so. A fine counter-argument is demonstrated time and again by the intercepted "chatter" that results in the raising or lowering of the Department of Homeland Security's National Threat Level. Undoubtedly, much of what is intercepted may be just that—chatter. But it is unlikely that it has all been such. Moreover, all human activity at some point is subject to fallibility and carelessness, as

---

[21] Ibid., 46.

[22] Bruce Berkowitz, *The New Face of War: How War will be Fought in the 21st Century*, New York NY, The Free Press, 2003, p 9.

[23] Ibid.

[24] Ibid.

demonstrated by Usama Bin Laden himself in 1998, when repeated use of his satellite phone allowed U.S. forces to target his position with Tomahawk missiles.[25] Apparently the attack was so close to killing him that Bin Laden instituted rigid protocols for future sat-phone use.

Nevertheless, the impact of globalization makes this critical factor, over all the others, the most difficult to target. Despite this fact, the tendency—perhaps the misconception—may be to hedge all bets by relying on U.S. technical superiority. After all, most would agree that technology is clearly a critical strength of the U.S. against nearly every imaginable opponent on the planet. As with the other critical factors discussed thus far, targeting command and control as a terrorist organization's center of gravity would prove inadequate in the long run in that global communication today is highly amorphous and easily reconstituted via low tech means.[26]

THE CRITICAL 'CRITICAL FACTOR' IS THE COG

Ideology. Nothing is more valuable to <u>any</u> organization, be it peaceful or criminal, than its message to its constituency—the support of its followers is the foundation upon which it grows. In the case of a global terrorist organization like Al Qa'eda, it is statements such as the powerful yet concise declaration set forth in Usama Bin Laden's 1998 "Fatwah Urging Jihad Against Americans" that unites nearly all of its constituent and non-constituent supporters in over 60 nations around the world. Bin Laden, like Saddam Hussein and Ayatollah Khomeini before him, has been extremely successful at identifying common grievances against the United States and other

---

[25] Roland Jacquard, *In the name of Osama Bin Laden; Global Terrorism and the Bin Laden Brotherhood*, Durham NC, Duke University Press, 2002, p 46.

[26] Ibid., 47.

moderate Muslim regimes[27], grievances that strike a cord across a great swath of Muslims throughout the world, most of whom are <u>not</u> extremists. Moreover, he has perverted religious text and doctrine to justify his actions,[28] and continues to cleverly use history to frame his arguments. For example, his October 7th, 2001 pronouncement of the "humiliation and disgrace that Islam has suffered for more than eighty years"[29] (coincident with the fall of the Ottoman Empire after World War I and rise of Western colonialism in the Muslim world) and eloquently stated in his earlier Fatwah:

> *"The Arabian Peninsula has never—since God made it flat, created its desert, and encircled it with seas—been stormed by any forces like the crusader armies now spreading in it like locusts, consuming its riches and destroying its plantations."[30]*

Time and again, the Western cultures either underestimate or fail to recognize altogether the important role history plays in Muslim societies today. In fact, Bin Laden's allusions to the humiliating breakup of the Ottoman Empire between Britain and France may be completely lost on Western audiences but is still very much a source of contention within the Muslim world. Additionally, the United States, largely unknown to the vast majority of Muslims even one hundred years ago, is widely viewed today as the successor to imperialist Great Britain and France, in no small part due to America's lead in developing (and perhaps exploiting) the Arab petroleum industry and of course continued oil-related trade. Though an economic boom to a relative few, the vast majority of Muslims have

---

[27] John L. Esposito, *Unholy War: Terror in the Name of Islam*, New York NY, Oxford University Press, 2002, p 153.

[28] Ibid., 153.

[29] Bernard Lewis, The Crisis of Islam: Holy War and Unholy Terror, New York NY, Modern Library, 2003, xv.

[30] Usama Bin Laden, "Fatwah Urging Jihad Against Americans," 1998.

seen their once preeminent civilization decline and fester in the shadow of Western-led globalization.

Usama Bin Laden's command of this sentiment is vital to the success of Al Qa'eda's message particularly in the application of the concept of *Jihad*. One of the basic tasks bequeathed to all Muslims by the Prophet Mohammed is jihad, meaning literally "striving" or "effort" but more often used in the context of a struggle (or fight).[31] Muslim faith maintains that the world is divided into two houses: *Dar-al-Islam*, the House of Islam, where Muslim governance and faith rule supreme; and *Dar-al-Harb*, the house of war, ruled by infidels. Put simply, jihad is characterized by the struggle between the two houses until, ideally, worldwide adoption of- or rule by the Muslim faith. It is in distorting and exaggerating this principle that radical Islamic fundamentalists, like their counterparts in nearly any other religion, find the necessary moral ammunition to attack the United States, its culture and its commerce with the Muslim world. Fundamentalists reject Islamic law regarding the "goals and means of *valid* jihad"[32] (proportionality and necessity, targeting of innocents, declaration of jihad can only come from the caliphate... do these rules of engagement sound familiar?) and routinely seize the right to declare illegitimate war in the name of Islam.[33]

Let there be no argument, Islam is one of the world's great religions,[34] having given dignity and meaning to as much as one fifth the world's population. It teaches tolerance and acceptance of other cultures and indeed other religions. However, like any

---

[31] Lewis, 31.

[32] Esposito, 157.

[33] Ibid., 157.

[34] Lewis, 25.

religion, it is subject to radical extremism that would see its values imposed involuntarily and foster unabated hatred for dissenting points of view. To this end, Al Qa'eda has, in essence, hijacked the Islamic faith in order to promote its own radical view, and will stop at nothing to see its mission through. Clearly Al Qa'eda's center of gravity is this ideology. The subjectivity of Muslim canon is its strength (through perversion and distortion) yet it is also its vulnerability. This distortion of Muslim belief is entirely vulnerable to dissection by legitimate Islamic scholars and theologians by exposing that "there is nothing Islamic about Al Qa'eda's power grab."[35] A critical first step for the United States in defeating global terrorism is to focus all of its instruments of national power on defeating this ideology of hate and intolerance. .

STRATEGIC ROADMAP TO SUCCESS

To be successful at winning the hearts and minds of the Muslim world, it will take a great deal of effort to become not only *much* more educated in Islamic law and practice, but also far more tolerant of the same. Though some have argued that this "clash of civilizations"[36] is the definitive mark of our time and here to stay, bridging the gap is not as impossible as it may seem. Indeed, there was a time during European colonial rule of the Middle East that the peoples there viewed the United States as the "beacon of democracy"[37] and a champion of human rights. However, that image has largely been shattered due to the massively widespread perception of unfairness and inconsistency in U.S. policies toward the Israeli/Palestinian conflict.[38] Many in the Muslim world see the

---

[35] 'Combating Terrorism in a Globalized World,' National War College, 2002, ch 2, p10.

[36] Samuel P. Huntington, *The Clash of Civilizations and the Remaking of World Order*, New York NY, Simon & Schuster, 1996, preface.

[37] 'Combating Terrorism in a Globalized World,' National War College, 2002, ch 7 p 4.

[38] Ibid.

U.S. espousal of inherent self-determination and human rights as "transparent or disingenuous"[39] when they witness hard-line treatment of rock throwing Arabs as opposed to little or no U.S. criticism of brutal Israeli policy in the West Bank and Gaza Strip. Such misbalanced policies only give Bin Laden popular support to pursue his agenda; "the [American's] aim is also to serve the Jews' petty state and divert attention from its occupation of Jerusalem and murder of Muslims there."[40] "There" is where the U.S. should begin its "war of ideas"[41] to start to win back over the hearts and minds, thereby deflating the cause of radical Islamic terrorism.

Step One: Show decisive leadership! Facilitate a peaceful end to the Israeli-Palestinian war. There is literally no greater uniting cause for Muslim peoples the world over than to see an end to the plight of Palestinians under the current Israeli occupation. The United States can no longer sit on the sidelines and passively watch both sides slowly annihilate each other. With each Palestinian suicide bomber hitting his (or her!) mark, and each Israeli air strike retaliating ten fold, and inciting further revenge from yet another Palestinian suicide bomber, the fate of the Jewish state marches ever closer to destruction, the Palestinian State marches further from realization and "America's image in the Middle East grows more and more poisoned,"[42] taking with it the credibility of the moderate Arab and Muslim nations who hold out support towards a peaceful settlement. Regardless of how many Palestinians Israel kills, it will not solve the two central problems: First, the Palestinian population explosion currently underway will certainly

---

[39] Esposito, 154.

[40] Usama Bin Laden, "Fatwah Urging Jihad Against Americans," 1998.

[41] Thomas L. Friedman, *Longitudes and Attitudes: The World in the Age of Terrorism*, New York NY, Anchor Press, 2003, p 180.

[42] Thomas L. Friedman, 'War of Ideas, Part 4', The New York Times, 18 Jan 2004.

lead to Israeli Muslims outnumbering Israeli Jews within a few years[43], and this fact

manifest in a democratic state could very well spell the end of the Jewish state

altogether.[44] Second, the explosion of Arab-run media (both satellite TV and the

Internet) throughout the Middle East and the world means that the images of the Intifada,

particularly Israel's heavy-handedness (justified or not) will be broadcast into Arab

homes. "If 100 million Arab-Muslims are brought up with these images, Israel will not

survive."[45] Furthermore, the continued status quo in Israel and the Palestinian territories

only serves to energize Usama Bin Laden's base. As a staunch ally of Israel, the desired

ally of Palestine and an avowed enemy of Bin Laden and Al Qa'eda, the United States

has the opportunity to help Israelis and Palestinians survive and prosper while at the same

time defeating the message of hate propagated by Usama and Al Qa'eda.

To accomplish this, some concrete strategic initiatives must be carried out at the

earliest opportunity. First, the U.S. should *unilaterally* grant full diplomatic recognition

to a free and independent State of Palestine based on UN-mandated borders. This

pronouncement should be repeatedly pronounced throughout the Western and Arab

media as just what it is—an unambiguous recognition of statehood—not a vision, not

wishful thinking, not something to negotiate on in the future. Second, Washington must

publicly demand a complete withdrawal of all Israeli military forces from newly-

recognized Palestine. Third, the U.S. must *publicly* demand Israel halt and dismantle all

its settlements in Palestine. Finally, follow these declarations by leading through

action— the U.S. should create from the ground up—and lead—a credible "transition

---

[43] Friedman, *Longitudes*, 143.

[44] Ibid.

[45] Ibid., 135.

structure to oversee the gradual [re]building of the Palestinian Authority and the gradual unbuilding of settlements,"[46] specifically a force under direct *U.S.-led* UN or NATO supervision. Such a bold *U.S.-led* initiative will not only guarantee the generation of responsible governance in Palestine[47], it will provide security for both Arabs and Israelis, and most importantly, demonstrate to the Muslim world that the United States will definitively use its instruments of power, including a willingness to commit its own blood to finally resolve this issue. Are we rewarding terrorism by doing this? Some may say so though the crimes themselves should <u>never</u> go unpunished. Nevertheless <u>this</u> issue must be dealt with *definitively* and *immediately* if we are to defeat the terrorists' popular message of hate.

Step Two: Cease "force-feeding" Western-styled governance where it is not ready or welcomed, and engage those nations where new ideas on Islamic democracy incubate. In 2001, Iranian president Mohammad Khatami best summed up the emerging view of Islamic democracy in noting that today's "existing democracies do not necessarily follow one formula"[48] no doubt in reference to democratic systems ranging from conservative federalism to socialist democracy. He stated further that "it may be a democracy with the inclusion of religious norms in government. We (the Islamic Republic) have accepted this option."[49] Though it is difficult to accept this premise from the leader of a nation with perhaps the most empowered religious

---

[46] Ibid., 179.

[47] Ibid.

[48] Esposito, 146.

[49] Ibid.

hardliners in the world, it nevertheless offers a ray of hope that there are *Muslims* that may agree, albeit somewhat, with our own basic democratic principles.

Ironically, President Khatami is a man the United States needs on its side as it fights its war on global terror. Not because his country could de-legitimize Hezbollah if it so chose (though that would be nice), but because his moderate philosophy on religion and government grows ever more popular with a growing majority of his people, and its propagation inside and outside Iran's borders could very well be a vital bridge between civilizations. Thomas Friedman brilliantly illustrates the ongoing debate "process" in Iran to find a better balance of state and religion; "People get arrested for speaking out, go to prison, write books, eventually get released, run for Parliament, speak out, start a reformist newspaper, and get arrested again."[50] This "crazy semi-democracy"[51] may incubate true democracy in Islam even before Saudi Arabia, America's closest ally in the Middle East, does.

Especially as the U.S. attempts to germinate a viable government in neighboring Iraq, it would do well to heed these growing pains going on next door in Iran. Iran has the most to contribute in this region, having borne witness to failed secular despotism under the Shah as well as failed religious despotism under the Ayatollahs.[52] Their moderation from above and below can show the United States it can accept a certain degree of theocratic government in its democratic model, and show Muslims throughout the world that it can accept a certain degree of democratic government in its theocratic model. With everyone happy, where will Bin Laden get his support then?

---

[50] Friedman, *Longitudes*, 188.

[51] Ibid.

[52] Ibid., 189.

Step Three: *Finally*, get out of the Middle East! Simply said, to the West, the Arabian Peninsula and its surroundings have a very obvious "mystique" about it. Then again, perhaps the greatest misdeed one can render upon another's religion is over-simplifying it. More appropriately, greater "Arabia" is more important to the followers of Islam than any other place is to any other group of people in the world. The point is, once the United States military has finished its part in righting some of the wrongs in the region, specifically those discussed above, it should leave… quickly! As long as foreign men and ships of war remain on or near the Muslim holy land, characters like Usama Bin Laden will *always* be able to conjure up images of the centuries-old Crusades. Moreover, for the United States in particular, its sole superpower status in the world means that the only effective tool an opposing force like Al Qa'eda has at its disposal is terrorism, either directly (as in attacking the *USS Cole*) or indirectly (as in attacking the U.S. homeland on September 11th, 2001). For once, the United States should take the proactive role of limiting globalization of its culture in a part of the world that either does not accept American culture as moral, or is not ready to accept it. Be cautioned, this is not an argument for rejecting modernity; rather it is an argument for not force-feeding modernity to the unwilling or unready. After all, it would not be deemed appropriate for the U.S. government to set up shop in the middle of Pennsylvania Hamish country and expect its inhabitants to start using cell phones. Nor should it be acceptable in the Middle East. The sooner we make that realization, and Muslims around the world *see* us make that realization, the sooner we will *not* be viewed as the new Crusaders.

CONCLUSION

It is hoped that despite a heavily strategic flavor, the reader sees that this paper has examined this war on terror through the lens of operational art. Several critical factors were named, those that were vulnerable were identified and a logical center of gravity was chosen to target. Many before have argued the significance of targeting a global terrorist network's command and control or finances. Many too have argued for leadership decapitation—indeed the American public has a long standing love-affair with nemeses. However, they all come back if the "beef" is still present... someone else takes up the cause, raises more money and thinks up new ways to carry their evil deeds out.

The campaign against Islamic terrorism is obviously the first step in the overall war, one where we have seen the military instrument used most visibly in Afghanistan and Iraq thus far. But more importantly, the United States must do more to employ the diplomatic, economic and informational instruments in order to debunk the false message Al Qa'eda disseminated throughout the Muslim world, that the United States with its armies and warships are waging a war against Islam. The U.S. must use its power to prove to one and a half billion Muslims that it is acting in their best interest and is not a threat to their religion and beliefs. It must do so through action and engagement, not sanctions and no-fly zones; through new thinking, not mirror imaging. With proper nourishment, Western and Islamic ideals can not only exist together but live symbiotically in a way the world has never seen. Only when this is realized will Bin Laden's hate-filled message fall on deaf ears and his brand of international terrorism fall into the ash heap of history.

BIBLIOGRAPHY

Berkowitz, Bruce. *The New Face of War: How War will be Fought in the 21ˢᵗ Century*, New York, NY: The Free Press, 2003.

Bin Laden, Usama. "Fatwah Urging Jihad Against Americans." Published in Al-Quds al-'Arabi, 23 Feb 1998.

Bodansky, Yossef. *Bin Laden: The Man Who Declared War on America*. New York NY: Prima, 2001.

Echevarria II, Antulio J. "Clausewitz's Center of Gravity: Changing Our Warfighting Doctrine—Again!" Strategic Studies Institute. U.S. Army War College, 2002. Accessed at: http://www.iwar.org.uk/military/resources/cog/gravity.pdf

Esposito, John L. *Unholy War: Terror in the Name of Islam*. New York NY: Oxford University Press, 2002.

Friedman, Thomas L. *Longitudes and Attitudes: The World in the Age of Terrorism*. New York, NY: Knopf, 2003.

_____. "War of Ideas, Part 4." The New York Times. 18 Jan 2004.

Housen, Roger T. "A Temple of Antiterrorism Strategy." Unpublished Research Paper, National Defense University: National War College, 2002.

Howard, Michael and Paret, Peter, eds. Translation of Carl Von Clausewitz, *On War*, Princeton NJ: Princeton University Press, 1976.

Huntington, Samuel P. *The Clash of Civilizations and the Remaking of World Order*. New York, NY: Simon & Schuster, 1996.

Jacquard, Roland. *In the name of Osama Bin Laden; Global Terrorism and the Bin Laden Brotherhood*, Durham, NC: Duke University Press, 2002

Kohn, Bryan S. "Attacking Islamic Terrorism's Strategic Center of Gravity." Unpublished Research Paper, U.S. Navy War College, 2002.

Lewis, Bernard. *The Crisis of Islam: Holy War and Unholy Terror*. New York, NY: The Modern Library, 2003.

Marguiles, Alexander. "A Strategy for Winning the 'War on Terrorism'." Unpublished Research Paper, National Defense University: National War College, 2002.

Pillar, Paul R. *Terrorism and U. S. Foreign Policy*. Washington, DC: The Brookings Institute Press, 2001.

Record, Jeffery. "Bounding the Global War on Terrorism." Strategic Studies Institute. U.S. Army War College, 2002.

Rielly, James. LTC, USMC. " A Strategic Level Center of Gravity Analysis on the Global War on Terrorism" Unpublished Research Paper, U.S. Army War College, 2002.

Student Task Force on Combating Terrorism. "Combating Terrorism in a Globalized World." National Defense University: National War College, 2002.

U.S. Department of State. *Patterns of Global Terrorism*, Washington DC, 2002.

U.S. President. *The National Security Strategy of the United States of America*. Washington, DC: 2002.

U.S. President. *National Strategy for Combating Terrorism*. Washington, DC: 2003.

Vego, Milan. *Operational Warfare*. Newport, RI: Naval War College, 2000.

www.ingramcontent.com/pod-product-compliance
Lightning Source LLC
Chambersburg PA
CBHW081817280526
45789CB00008B/3139